Empathy

Empathy

Gaurav Malhotra

GenNext Publication

First Published, 2018

Published by

GenNext Publication
5, Ansari Road
Daryaganj, New Delhi-110002
Phone: 9811692060
E-mail: gennextpublication@hotmail.com

Printed at: G. Print Process, Delhi.

Cataloging in Publication Data—DK
Courtesy: D.K. Agencies (P) Ltd. <docinfo@dkagencies.com>

Malhotra, Gaurav, author.
Empathy / Gaurav Malhotra.
pages cm
1 ISBN: 978-93-5324-122-3

1. Terrorism. I. Title.

LCC HV6431.M35 2018 | DDC 303.625 23

PREFACE

This book is about those who believe that humanity still exist in this world, it is all about truth that is kept away from the reach of the common man. This book does not point towards any individual, or society or any government. On a major note, this book is against terrorism but in favour of those who are forced into it.

INTRODUCTION

"war is not won with soldiers
It is won with belief"

"history is written by victors not
necessarily by heroes"

Gaurav Malhotra

EMPATHY

The word shows about its own meaning that the world is not big enough to be empathised by someone to some other person, but to know the facts that we all think we already know. Empathising something does not mean that you are changing something, it only shows the real stage of experiences that the other person would be feeling or would have felt particular at that point of time. Kindly note that this book is not to hurt the sentiments or values of any religion or a nation. To remove the hindrances of enforcing Human RIGHTS IN EVERY country as one is the basic need in today's world. We all know that the world is changing day by day and so shall we should, this is why it is mandatory for us to empathise others values, experiences and other dominations in this era. It is believed that we all are one and must have equal rights. But what about different nations having different rules and different enforcement of rights on different people. We all KNOW that America is a world power and Russia was sometime a World Power. But at the time of Soviet - Afghanistan war (1979-1989) US Supplied Arms and Ammunitions to the Afghanistan to fight the Russia during the period of Cold War. Osama Bin Laden was indirectly or directly created by the US itself to fight against Russian troops in Afghanistan. But on the emerge of 2001 everything changed, the US was attacked by the Laden as we all know. But this book is not about exposing or blaming a nation, but to understand the dominance of some wealthy nations on the weaker ones. To stop this we have to join our hands to make some difference. Innocent people are dying in these weak countries just because they are the citizens of such countries ? Just because they were born there? Is this we call the Human Rights? No. Absolutely not. Its always made look the blames are indirectly made through these weaker countries because of which many Civilians die every year. Whether this nation or that, people die due to raids by the Wealthier Countries or due to the failure of government in the weaker countries.

Terrorist, Terrorism, who created these words, who

created them. We did. How ? Just by believing those who wanted us to do so. Who wanted ? Those who are benefited through such kind of terrorist attacks. Terrorist attacks always have motives behind them, no, don't you think that they have religious motives. Yes they might seem like they have direct religious motives but they are indirectly motivated by the big guns of *wealthy nations. Why and what kind of benefit could one have through a terrorist attack. Ok, lets say A is a person who is a business man and owns and runs a big company named A Inc., now he has a competitor company named B Inc. which is having a key person named B. If B dies, B Inc. will suffer huge losses and on the other hand A Inc. will indirectly be benefited as a major part of the* business market will shift towards the A Inc., making huge profits for A say $ 1000 Million. So, A plans an attack to kill B and in order to do so A plans in three ways:

1. A goes to BJ kills him, Enquiry is set by the Government and A is caught.
2. A offers $ 600 Million to the terrorist group and

asks to plan a blast when B is at a Public Place and the terrorist group takes the responsibility of the attack by killing 20 people including B, so that no enquiry is conducted particularly for BJs death and A is never caught.

3. A plans a bomb blast in such an order that few other people are also killed so that particularly B's

death is not investigated. A plans a bomb blast at a public place and when B arrives, the Bomb is exploded and as it was on a public place a total of 20 people die including B. On the same time A contacts a terrorist group and asks them to just take the responsibility of the attack offering $ 200 Million, so that it may look like a terrorist attack and no enquiries are done to catch A. Instead of catching A everyone gets busy looking for the Terrorist group.

Oh, come on, government believes those who are criminals sitting at a distant place, by just the fact that they took responsibility of the incidence?

Instead of this the Government shall conduct enquiry for the incidence, without considering the fact that it was a terrorist attack and shall catch the main criminal who is hiding behind the **terrorism veil. Terrorism Veil,** here is defined as the shelter to criminal activities done by some other but the responsibility is taken by the Terrorist groups so that the main person behind the incidence is never caught or even noticed as the government just gets busy in catching the terrorist group.

It is very shocking that sometimes A here is a key person of government of a nation and B could be the key person of other nation's government. So, even the Nations use this type of Terrorism Veil.

In fact, around 10 per cent of the fund to the terrorist groups comes directly from the government which is busy raging a war against them. Twenty per cent from other countries, 60 per cent from private businessmen and 10 per cent from few religious groups.

So, in order to stop major funding of the Terrorist groups, the government and its authorities must start setting up enquiries for the attack treating as if it is not conducted by any terrorist group and catch the main criminal behind the incidence, so that these kind of financial transactions are stopped and the Terrorist groups gets financially weaker.

Finance and Manpower are the two main shoulders of the Terrorist Organisations. Lets now move on to the Manpower they get from. Manpower, is itself a strong word which depicts the power and use of the most powerful creature on this planet, Man. It is the main source and one of the main pillars of Terrorism. Some manpower comes from the religious groups, some are forced into it and some are misguided. It is very important for us to stop the main source of Manpower to such terrorist organisations. It can be done through spreading Education and necessities of life in those countries where such terrorist groups are active. With the spreading of Education and necessities of life the terrorist groups will be restricted from hiring these unpaid manpower.

For instance, say a village has such villagers that cannot even support basic necessities of life such as food and can't even afford Education for their children, the terrorist groups go to such villagers and ask them to give one child out of two or three in their family and take a little amount of money in return and they are told by the terrorist groups that they will send their child to heaven. In exchange of a little money that can buy their family necessities of life like food and a dream of heaven for their sacrificed child, they agree to such terrorist organisations.

If someone else could have provided the basic necessities of life to the villagers who are giving their children to the terrorist groups then, this manpower supply to these terrorist groups could have been stopped yet. Instead of this we all are making them more weaker by just secluding these countries and they are getting more poor. Children are misguided since beginning of their adolescence and treated as weapons to fight, taught only what the terrorist organisations *teach them. Just imagine it is not these children's fault if they kill someone when they become elder, as they know that this is right according to their upbringings, they do not know anything, they are innocent.* ***The cruelty lies in ignoring proper support for education of these children,*** *who become future terrorists.*

I don't know what to say about this, its not that anyone

is not aware what has to be done, just the fact is that everyone is waiting for someone else to step up and do something in this regard. Why ? Is it because we are cowards, we don't have time from our daily schedule? Yes, I do agree that we are cowards and we don't get time, so ? Is that it ? We will keep on waiting for them to come close to us and destroy our families? Or, we will come together to take a step for the establishment of effective education system for these Children, who are misguided by the different groups?

Please read this book forward if you agree till this, if not kindly give a request of Refund on the mentioned Website address at the end of this book. I hope you agree if you are still reading this, so now we have agreed all together that *we need to establish basic education system for these Children and give them at least basic education so that they can decide what is right and what is wrong. At least then we can fully blame them that they are terrorists. Lets join hands and try to provide a healthy atmosphere for basic amenities and adequate education system for the child whom can be* guided by us that how he can choose not to become a terrorist.

Time once gone, doesn't comes back. Take the decision on the right time so that we may not regret it in the near future. This is why we have to take a step that these structures that are created must be abolished so that no more soul on this earth cries for their family, for their children and loved ones just because of some mere person wants that just in order to spread terror or any personal motives. The ISIS is raised by which country or United Countries, we all know. Don't worry time will come and tell the truth as the most powerful thing on this universe is TIME.

But when that time will come there will be no hidden truth, what will happen then. For that we need to know the truth and that is after World

War II due to so much loss of man and material, the nations which do not wanted that World War III should happen, they decided a solution to Unite the whole world. Uniting different countries is a big job and a difficult one too. But if they all are given a common enemy, then it would be easy to unite them.

So this is what they did. They created the word Terrorism.

Terrorism and Terrorist groups emerged and they gave themselves to the world as common enemy and united the world. But at what sake? Of not having a World War again? Well, this might be an efficient and effective way to unite the world but not ethical and human at all.

With the removal of Terrorism, the whole world will lose a common enemy, the

World may not remain United and Breaking out of World War has a bigger chance. But, what will you choose ? Children being shot being in School by a Terrorist Group or a World War and dying in Patriotism?

Now lets stop this. What are we waiting for ? We all know that this Terrorism is fake created and is even getting worse day by day. I personally did'nt liked the incident of

Black Day at Pakistan, where children were killed by a terrorist group in a school. Why? They were innocent and did'nt even knew who the men were and why were they killing them. Why small children ? This is completely not fare. This will surely bring the curse on the Humanity. They were not even aware what dying means. They were just screaming help, help and hiding beneath the desks that they used to study on, thinking that the desk will save their lives. But it did'nt. Some of them were asking that uncle why are you shooting on us ? Some of them were shouting and calling their parents Mom and Dad please come and save us.

And what are we doing? What are we doing ? Nothing. If we all decide then such things can never exist. Tactically, we must take appropriate steps and if each and every person will just take out only one hour out of their busy schedule, just one hour in an year, then this evil of terrorism can no longer be in existence. You know how to take out that one hour in an year. But what to do, just take a note, Whatever specialty you have just focus it into the removal of Terrorism, whether typing solutions on your Face Book wall or Tweet or just go out and talk about this to your known to ones. Only one Hour in a year can save millions of lives that are destroyed by Terrorist Groups. Or if you can't do this, help us do. We Empathy will approach the big guns of a nation to change their policies in this area, so that the lives can be saved. There are lot of other common enemies that the World can be united upon *and fight together and not only terrorism.*

- *The history is written by victors not by hero.*
- *To unite two together, give them a common enemy.*
- *End of Terrorism, can be the beginning of World War III.*
- *To unite the World, common enemy terrorism is given.*

Each and every human has the right to live free. Why not ? because they cannot take it like that. Just because they have to rule each and every possible moment that comes in geo politics. Geo politics is really a vast subject and to understand it one needs to think without the boundaries of the nations and even without the boundaries of any religion. Well, this is the reason why anyone who tries to think outside these boundaries are either with them or does not exist anymore. All this is an event that is going on just to ignore world war three, but according to me this is world war 16th that is going on in the world as the war fought on natural resources or on oil in which each and every country is involved, is also a world war. But yes of course weapons of mass destruction are not used, as the definition of weapons of mass destruction has been changed from nuclear weapons to terrorist organizations. To explain further, we can use the propaganda of involving some big identity and his visits to certain areas of the world. What came into your mind? the thing that might have come in your mind is thinking about a big political or a business figure *having links to places like the middle east nations. Just this is what I'm trying to say that each and every person has been made to draw his attention towards this particular area of the world. Why ? What are they trying to hide, why is our attention being drawn towards all this terrorism. Why is everyone after these terrorist organizations, why in our minds it is always entered that* these are your villains and these are the heroes of the world, they are trying to save this world and all that shit. Why is no body thinking of who are funding these organizations and why are they doing it. The root cause does not lye in "who is funding?", the root cause is "why is anyone funding these organizations ?" and for what benefit. Each and every person has the right to get benefits on his investments, but we can figure it out, we can give them the best alternatives to generate benefits. They do not have to create any terrorist organizations for any benefits. It is so stupid to do that. It is my warning to those who play with religions and even with the life of a human being. What would I do? Nothing. But what we all can do? Everything.

It is definitely not about stopping someone from doing anything. It is about understanding what is happening around you. "Acceptance is always better than retaliation", because through acceptance we can move forward and through this whatever might be the problem it no longer remains a problem itself. We just change the definition of that particular problem in minds and after we *accept it slowly and gradually that strategy of doing anything like creating and maintaining terrorist organizations, would no longer be required, we can just simply move forward by accepting what is happening around us. But, we must know the root cause and what is that? "why is anyone funding these organizations ?"*